Praise fo

With few Bible studies specially designed for parents raising children with special needs, *Held* is a much-welcomed resource for those who are struggling. Theologically sound and genuinely tender, Sandra and Lee Peoples effectively tie parents' own challenges to those who encountered God during Bible times. Study participants are left with far more than temporal solutions to life's daily challenges. They are encouraged to trust in God's plan as they learn from heroes of the faith. Parents give themselves a lasting gift by embracing *Held*.

Barbara Dittrich
Author *Special Studies for Special Parents Series*
Executive Director, SNAPPIN' MINISTRIES
(www.snappin.org)

I wish that I could adequately express how excited I am for this new book! For any parent who has a child with special needs and feels as if life is out of control, this book is for you. More than advice, *Held*, will give you the power of God's Word. This first of a kind bible-study for special needs parents is packed with Scripture-based references for the tough questions and more. More importantly, the study questions throughout this book will help you to take the truths of God's Word and apply them to your special-needs journey.

Simply put, this is a book for every parent. Every parent whose heart has been fractured by special needs. Every parent who feels alone and who needs strength for the special needs journey. Every parent who needs to find their way back to hope.

Mike Woods
Director Special Friends Ministry at First Baptist Orlando
Managing Editor of Not Alone Parents
(www.specialneedsparenting.net)

With *Held*, Sandra and Lee have done an amazing job of ministering to families of children with special needs, a group that often feels unnoticed, lonely, and misunderstood. They shared of themselves—joys, triumphs, trials, and pain—to let us know they understand where we are, what our lives are like. And then they invite Jesus into the picture and remind us how He responded to fears, disappointments, and pain with His amazing love.

Lee and Sandra don't offer clichés and pat answers. The issues faced by special needs families are too complex for that. What they do offer is hope, encouragement, and support for the journey. This is a Bible study I will turn to time and again and will definitely recommend to others!

Jennifer Janes, jenniferajanes.com

Navigating this world of special-needs parenting is foggy at best. We spend our lives on bended knee and in waiting rooms, looking for wisdom from white collars and white coats. We long for community, friends to walk with, family to celebrate and carry us. Oh, but this journey is quiet and lengthy. It changes with the seasons and even hours. Our maps are out of date with every new study and milestone.

Held comes at a time in my life when I am more confident with speech flash cards than Scripture memory. It is a beautiful, honest walk through God's Word with a keen focus on the extra-special lives we are cultivating at home. Sandra and Lee have given us the perspective of both a mom and a pastor. It is, finally, a legend to our map. A directional to the faith behind the life we lead and the long road ahead.

It is both a reference and guide written in our special-needs language, pointing to the cross. May it lead me ... and you ... ever closer.

Katie Mulder
Dayspring (in)courage community leader and special-needs mom, author of the Apple Pie, Anyone? journal at texasnorth.com, and Believer in miracles

Held: Learning to Live in God's Grip

A Bible Study for Special-Needs Parents

Lee and Sandra Peoples

All Scripture quotations are taken from *The Holy Bible, English Standard Version*, copyright © 2001 by Crossway Bibles, a division of Good News Publishers. Used by permission. All rights reserved.

ISBN-13: 978-1492391968
ISBN-10: 1492391964

Cover Design by Phil & Erin Ulrich,
Design by Insight (www.designbyinsight.net)
Layout by Teri Lynne Underwood,
terilynneunderwood.com
Edited by Terri Poss

Contents

Introduction

On November 16, 2010, our lives changed with just a short sentence from a child psychologist who had watched our three-year-old son interact with a speech therapist, an occupational therapist, and herself for the last hour. "We believe he has autism," she said. For us, that was the end and the beginning. Everything changed.

How we related to our parents and siblings changed. How we related to our friends changed. How we decorated (and safety-proofed) our home changed. What we ate changed. The doctor we saw changed (and changed, and changed, and changed again). Our plans for his education changed. Our budget changed. Our vacation plans changed. The books we read changed. What we needed from our church family changed. And even the way we viewed and related to God changed.

The changes weren't all bad. Most were good. God sanded off areas of disbelief and idolatry in our lives. He met our needs in His time and in His ways. We felt His presence. We knew He had not lost His grip on our lives.

The special-needs world wasn't new to us when our son got his autism diagnosis—Sandra's older sister Syble has Down syndrome, so Sandra has been in a special-needs family her entire life. She grew up going to Special Olympic events and hearing her parents talk about IEP meetings. She felt the stares when her family would go out to eat. Sandra even remembers being eight years old and asking God why Syble was born with a disability.

Those of us in the special-needs world ask tough questions. We are in tough situations. But God is faithful. Through His Word and the ministry of the Holy Spirit, He answers our questions. He brings us comfort and strength. Though this study, we will talk about some tough issues, like why God allows suffering, why some are born with disabilities, and how to act when others just don't understand your struggles.

When we minister to special needs families, we tell them what we needed to hear when we got James's diagnosis—you are not alone.

In this Bible study, you will learn you are not alone. You are in God's grip. He is in control of everything, even when life feels out of control. You will learn there is a future hope we all can cling to. You will learn there are others out there, just like you, who need to be shown they are also in the grip of God.

Held is designed to be done alone, as a couple, or with a group. There are questions throughout each chapter that will help you think about the material and apply what you learn. We are excited about what God will teach you through this study. As we wrote it, we learned so much. We are praying for you. We are praying for your family. Thank you for taking the first step to remembering God never loses His grip on you.

"For I, the Lord your God, hold your right hand; it is I who say to you, 'Fear not, I am the one who helps you'" (Isaiah 41:13).

In Order to Be in His Grip, You Need to Experience His Love

How can we speak with confidence about being in God's grip? We have experienced His love. Romans 5:8 says, "God shows his love for us in that while we were still sinners, Christ died for us." We believe all have sinned and fall short of God's glory (Romans 3:23). Sin leads to death, but God made a way, "the free gift of God is eternal life in Christ Jesus our Lord" (Rom. 6:23). When we admit we have sinned, we can ask God to forgive us and redeem us through the power of Christ's death, burial, and resurrection. Then, "we too might walk in newness of life" (Rom. 6:4).

This is where it all begins. Greg Lucas, author of *Wrestling with an Angel*, talks about his now young adult son Jake who has multiple diagnoses, including cerebral palsy, seizure disorder, and autism. Jake changed his dad's life. "When people ask me how I became a follower of Jesus, I always tell them a two-year-old, nonverbal, mentally disabled, autistic boy led me straight to the cross and since then has been used to display God's grace in the most amazing ways."[i]

Are you ready to stop living in your own power and learn to live in God's grip? Are you ready to follow Greg's example and allow your child and your circumstances to draw you to the cross? We ask you to email us at held@sandrapeoples.com so we can follow-up with you and connect you to a church in your area that can disciple you.

Chapter 1
You Are in His Grip

When our oldest son David was born, he was breathing too quickly. In the delivery room, we got to pass him around to the grandparents and ooh and ah over him, but only for a few minutes. The doctor wanted to monitor his heartbeat and slow his breathing. He was hooked up to the monitor and put in an incubator in the newborn nursery. Soon after, the grandparents went home and Sandra fell asleep, but Lee walked down the hall to the nursery to see David. The nurses said his breathing was still fast and he was restless and fussy. They let Lee stick his hand in the incubator to touch David. As soon as David felt his daddy's finger on the back of his hand, he was still. He was calm. And for the first of probably hundreds of times, Lee whispered, "Daddy's here. I've got you."

As David grows, there are more opportunities for Lee to whisper in his ear, "Daddy's here. I've got you." When David climbs in our bed after a big clap of thunder. When it's time to take off the training wheels. When they nervously stand in line for a roller coaster ride. Daddy is there. David can reach out his hand and find his daddy's hand waiting to grip his.

God Knows You and Holds You: Psalm 139

Just as David is comforted by Lee's presence, we are comforted by God's presence in our lives. We are held in His grip. Psalm 139 describes how David learned to trust God's grip. David addressed how much God knows, how close God is to him, and the power God possesses. Notice how these attributes are not vague qualities of God, but are active qualities. Psalm 139 shows us God is all knowing, always there, and all powerful. This psalm teaches an important truth—you are in God's grip.

Read these verses from Psalm 139:

O LORD, you have searched me and known me!
2 You know when I sit down and when I rise up;
  you discern my thoughts from afar.
3 You search out my path and my lying down
  and are acquainted with all my ways.
4 Even before a word is on my tongue,
  behold, O LORD, you know it altogether.
5 You hem me in, behind and before,
  and lay your hand upon me.
6 Such knowledge is too wonderful for me;
  it is high; I cannot attain it.

7 Where shall I go from your Spirit?
  Or where shall I flee from your presence?
8 If I ascend to heaven, you are there!

If I make my bed in Sheol, you are there!
⁹ If I take the wings of the morning
   and dwell in the uttermost parts of the sea,
¹⁰ even there your hand shall lead me,
    and your right hand shall hold me.
¹¹ If I say, "Surely the darkness shall cover me,
    and the light about me be night,"
¹² even the darkness is not dark to you;
    the night is bright as the day,
    for darkness is as light with you.

¹³ For you formed my inward parts;
    you knitted me together in my mother's
womb.
¹⁴ I praise you, for I am fearfully and
wonderfully made.
Wonderful are your works;
    my soul knows it very well.
¹⁵ My frame was not hidden from you,
when I was being made in secret,
    intricately woven in the depths of the earth.
¹⁶ Your eyes saw my unformed substance;
in your book were written, every one of them,
    the days that were formed for me,
    when as yet there was none of them.

¹⁷ How precious to me are your thoughts, O God!
    How vast is the sum of them!
¹⁸ If I would count them, they are more than the
sand.
    I awake, and I am still with you.

²³ Search me, O God, and know my heart!
   Try me and know my thoughts!
²⁴ And see if there be any grievous way in me,
   and lead me in the way everlasting!

How well do you know yourself? This sounds like a silly question, of course you know yourself well. You know what you like to eat, what television shows you like to watch, what vacation spots you like, your favorite color, etc. You know yourself pretty well. If you were asked if anyone else knows you better than you know yourself, you might quickly respond no. Actually, there is someone else who knows you better than you — God.

? Psalm 139 teaches God knows us better than we even know ourselves. Look at what David said about God in verses 1-3. Let's list the actions of God we see in these verses:

verse 1, "You have _____ me,"

verse 2, "You _____ my sitting down and my rising up,"

verse 3, "you _____ my thoughts,"

verse 3, "You _____ my path."

That is intimate knowledge. Nothing is hidden. Hebrews 4:13 says "No creature is hidden from his sight, but all are naked and exposed to the eyes of him to whom we must give an account."

Notice what God does with this knowledge. In Psalm 139:5 David declared, "You have hedged me behind and before, and laid Your hand upon me." Simply put—God had David in His grip. God held David up and gave David reassurance of His presence with him.

? We know from studying the life of David, he understood suffering. What stories of suffering do you remember from David's life? List some here:

Here are a few we thought of:

He ran for his life when Saul was after him (1 Samuel 19, 21, 23 and other instances)

He didn't always get along with his wife Michal (2 Samuel 6)

One child died when he was just days old (2 Samuel 12)

His son Absalom tried to overthrow his father's reign and Absalom died (2 Samuel 15 and 2 Samuel 18)

During those times, David may have felt he had slipped from God's grip. He may have worried God was absent from his life.

As special-needs parents, we can feel scared. We don't know why we're going through hard times. We don't know if or when they will end. We don't know what will happen next. We toss and turn at night. We don't want to get the bills in the mail. We don't want to answer the phone when the doctor calls. But pastor and author Pete Wilson writes, "We don't really have a fear problem. We have a faith problem. We've lost confidence that our heavenly Father will take care of us … even those of us who have trusted our heavenly Father with our eternities often have a tough time trusting him with our tomorrows."[ii]

🄯 Can you recall a time you were scared? How did God calm your fears?

Two Responses to Suffering

People have two basic responses when they
suffer: they worship God or they walk away
from God. As a pastor, Lee has seen both choices
in the lives of people. He has seen people get
crushing news—a husband tragically die, or a
wife get cancer—and he has seen them still
worship God. He has also seen some people lose
a job, lose their home, or lose their health, and
watched them walk away and want nothing to
do with God. "When life doesn't turn out the
way you thought it was going to turn out, you
may think you're losing control. But the truth is,
you never had control in the first place. The only
thing you do control is how you respond to your
disappointments and your unexpected obstacles.
And here you have some options."[iii]

     What was David's response to all the
tragedies in his life? In verse 7 he asked two
questions, "Where can I go from Your Spirit?"
and "Where can I flee from Your presence?"
There are two ways we can understand what
David said here. First, we can read those verses
as David saying, "I want to flee from you, but I
realize there is no where I can go to get away
from your presence." Second, we can
understand David saying, "God, thank you, that
no matter where I go, you are there." Since
David doesn't give us the original intent, both
interpretations can be true. There is no where we

can flee from God, and that should lead us to celebrate, to praise Him!

Learning to live in God's grip means learning God is with you at all times and there is no where you will go where God is not with you. This means when you face a tough doctor's appointment, a tough IEP meeting, or a tough day at home, He is with you. God is present and we cannot escape His presence.

❓ How do these words from David's psalm bring you comfort?

God Holds You in the Storms

In the book of Matthew, a story from the life of Jesus also reminds us we are in His grip. After Jesus fed five thousand men by multiplying five loaves of bread and two fish, He sent His disciples out in a boat while He dismissed the crowds and prayed alone. Matthew 14:23 says, "When evening came, he was there alone, but the boat by this time was a long way from the land, beaten by the waves, for the wind was against them." Some of His disciples—Peter, Andrew, James, and John—were experienced fishermen. They earned their living out on the seas. But from the description in Matthew, that storm sounded like it would have even scared the most experienced among them. As they were being tossed around by the wind, Jesus came to them, walking on the sea. The disciples were terrified, but Jesus said to them, "Take heart; it is I. Do not be afraid" (v. 27).

But then something unexpected happened. "And Peter answered him, 'Lord, if it is you, command me to come to you on the water'" (v. 28). Not many of us would have volunteered to step out of the boat. Maybe Peter the fisherman had been dreaming of this opportunity his entire life. His father was also a fisherman, so he grew up around the water. Did he ever step onto the shore to see how lightly he could touch the water before he got wet? Did he study the buoyancy of the boat and wonder how many fish he could add to it before it started to sink? Did he see Jesus walking on the water and think, "Here's my chance!"?

Jesus told Peter to come and Peter got out of the boat, walked on the water, and approached Jesus. "But when he saw the wind, he was afraid and beginning to sink he cried out, 'Lord, save me.' Jesus immediately reached out his hand and took hold of him, saying to him, 'O you of little faith, why did you doubt?'" (vv. 30–31). Peter's thoughts could have been something like this, "I'm *walking* on water. I'm walking *on water*. Wait, I'm *walking on water*?!"

But then Jesus reached out. He grabbed on. He took hold. Walking and sinking — they weren't just Peter's actions anymore. Christ was with him. They were so close that Jesus was acting on behalf of Peter. His strength was Peter's strength. His power was Peter's power. As Jesus held Peter in His grip, Peter was able to do something only Christ Himself had the ability to do—walk on water.

What happened next? They got into the boat, the wind ceased, "And those in the boat worshiped him, saying, 'Truly you are the Son of God'" (v. 33).

? Has there been a time you stepped out in faith and then got scared?

(Example from our lives: We felt God calling us to adopt from Ethiopia. But because we're a single-income household, we were required to raise $15,000 in ninety days to prove we would have the finances to complete the adoption. We stepped out in faith and said yes to adopting, but were scared we couldn't raise the money in time.)

? Read verse 33 again and notice the response of those in the boat:

Worship was the result! Just like we saw in the Psalm by David. When you know, when you truly believe, when you experience being in God's grip, you worship. You say with David, "I praise you … wonderful are your works" (Psalm 139:14).

God Will Give You More Than You Can Handle

When you heard your child's diagnosis, some well-meaning friend may have tried to console you with the common Christian cliché, "God won't give you more than you can handle." That's simply not true. Abraham couldn't handle killing his son. Moses couldn't handle leading God's people across the Red Sea. Esther couldn't handle approaching the king to beg for her peoples' lives. Daniel couldn't handle the lion's den. They were called to challenges they couldn't overcome on their own.

Pete Wilson writes, "One of the characteristics I have noticed about the Plan B situations in my life is that they often require more of me than I think I have."[iv] It is true you cannot handle your current situation on your own.

▣ Let's look up the following verses and see what else is true:

Hebrews 13:5:

John 16:33

Psalm 9:9

Because these promises are true, you can overcome obstacles. You can face fears. You can find rest. Romans 8:37–39 says, "Now, in all these things we are more than conquerors through him who loved us. For I am sure that neither death nor life, nor angels nor rulers, nor things present nor things to come, nor powers, nor height nor depth, nor anything else in all creation, will be able to separate us from the love of God in Christ Jesus our Lord." Nothing can separate you from His love. Nothing can take you from His grip.

Chapter 2
When You're Searching

Story from Sandra

One of the first issues we wanted to tackle after James's autism diagnosis was his stomach pain. He was severely constipated. Armed with intuition, tenacity, and research from the books, I called James's pediatrician's office and explained James's symptoms to one of the doctors on staff. I said I would like to run a stool yeast culture and microscopic exam. He said I was "clearly uneducated and uninformed."

He explained how the Internet works, telling me that anyone can publish anything on the World Wide Web; it didn't even have to be true. That's why the Internet is dangerous for *people like me*. We get an idea in our heads and "chase a white rabbit."

He said the test was not "cost effective" and ultimately refused to run it for us. He said we needed to look at real science and not unproven theories. He assured me it wasn't a yeast issue, and gave me the name of a well-respected pediatric gastroenterologist in our area. I was dumbfounded at how he treated me and how he so easily dismissed my research (from books, not the Internet as he suggested). I said, "Thank you for your time," hung up the phone, and cried.

It took a few weeks to get an appointment with the well-respected pediatric gastroenterologist. One cold day in February, the entire family drove an hour away to meet with him. We waited for thirty minutes in the lobby. We waited another hour in the examination room. The nurse was sympathetic and encouraging as I answered her questions about James. "I'm sure the doctor will be able to help him," she said, "He's helped so many children."

The doctor finally came in our exam room and asked a few questions, interrupting my explanations and theories. When I told him I thought James had a yeast overgrowth, he completely ignored me. Even though he had been looking in my eyes as I spoke, he didn't acknowledge that I had said anything.

He turned his attention to James, and, after pushing on James's stomach, he simply told us to use a stool softener (even though we told him that eliminating dairy from James's diet and adding probiotics and prunes each day had been helpful) and come back to see him in six weeks. He assured us he had seen many children who were simply constipated like James, and a little stool softener was all he needed. When was regular again, he would be fine. When we got in the car, I looked at Lee and said, "We aren't doing what he said. I know it's more than just constipation. We aren't coming back to see him. We need to find another doctor who will help us."

We continued to seek help for James's digestive issues. I decided to call another doctor in the pediatric practice we used to see if he would order the stool analysis. But I lost my nerve. I put it off and put it off. Finally I asked Lee to do it. This was one of those times I needed him to do something I just couldn't do. The previous doctors had almost made me lose faith in the entire system. I didn't want to be told I was "uneducated and uninformed" again. And I didn't want to be ignored.

Lee made an appointment with the third doctor. To prepare for this visit, I took a video of James straining to have a bowel-movement. He held onto the arm of a chair, cocked one leg, and cried and screamed as he strained. We had learned we couldn't pick him up to comfort him when he did this, or he would stop trying which would make it worse for him. I thought if the doctor could just see the pain he was in, he would agree something more was wrong than what a stool-softener could fix.

Lee took James to the appointment because I had to work. This doctor was kind and listened, but he said he didn't know enough about the test to order it. He did order stool sample tests from the local lab for parasites. At least we could eliminate a possible cause with this test. The tests came back and James did not have parasites. But he still had all the symptoms of yeast overgrowth. We prayed for healing. We prayed for wisdom. We prayed for a Plan D.

Our behavioral therapist, Pam, has a son with autism. I asked her which doctor she used and she gave me his contact information. I called to schedule an appointment for James, but they said they had to see his records before they would accept him as a patient. I called the boys' pediatrician and requested the records be transferred. This process took weeks. They said they sent them but the new doctor never received them. We finally had to pick up the records ourselves and drive them to the new doctor, nearly an hour away. Then we waited weeks to get an appointment with the new doctor. The morning of James's appointment finally came and we drove to the new doctor's office. I had researched yeast overgrowth again, and was prepared to list James's symptoms and ask for the test. This research convinced me even more that James was suffering from yeast overgrowth.

We arrived at the office and Lee went to the window to give them our insurance information. We have primary insurance and James has secondary insurance, provided by the state. When I had talked to the receptionist at this office and he asked about our insurance, I mentioned our primary insurance only and he said they accepted it. But when we showed up that day for the appointment, we found out this doctor did not take James's secondary insurance. We offered to just pay the co-pay and not file with the secondary insurance but they, by law, could not let us do that.

Lee was angry. I was sad. We asked for the copy of the boys' medical records before we left since it took so long to get them transferred. I sent Lee and the boys to the car and waited in the lobby, crying. I told one of the receptionists, "Our son is autistic and we heard this doctor was kind. We just want a doctor who listens and is kind." They were sympathetic, but there was nothing they could do.

We drove an hour back home in silence, except for Lee asking "Do you want to talk about it?" and me saying, "Not yet." It was one of the many times we've had to give each other space and grace.

At the end of our list of options, we decided it was time to find a DAN (Defeat Autism Now) doctor. My Internet search led me to Dr. Richard Layton in Baltimore, Maryland. In early September 2011 we met with Dr. Layton and talked about James in detail for over an hour. I had filled out the paper work ahead of time and made a note of my expectations at the bottom—we wanted James's stomach to work better. Dr. Layton asked, "Is this your only goal? Just to make his stomach better?" I said, "Well, I've been hurt and ignored by doctors for the last year. If nothing else happens as a result of our visit, I want his tummy to feel better." Dr. Layton said, "I think we can do a lot more than that."

? Have you been in a situation that required you to search for a solution? Think back to the places you looked and how long the search took. Did you find a solution or are you still searching?

Finally Finding Relief

In Mark 5, we meet a woman who had tried to find relief from many doctors. "And there was a woman who had had a discharge of blood for twelve years, and who had suffered much under many physicians, and had spent all that she had, and was no better but rather grew worse" (vv. 25–26).

We can relate! Like so many of us who have tried doctors, therapies, supplements, diets, and tests, this woman was weary. No one could help her. And her issue wasn't just a physical one. Because she was constantly bleeding, she was considered unclean. According to Levitical law, she would have to stay away from others, including her family.

But she had heard reports of Jesus. She knew His reputation as a healer. She was desperate enough to risk touching others and being shamed to get close enough, "For she said, 'If I touch even his garments, I will be made well.' And immediately the flow of blood dried up, and she felt in her body that she was healed of her disease" (vv. 28–29). Relief at last! No more blood. No more loneliness. No more weariness.

Could she sneak away through the crowd as unnoticed as she came? "But Jesus, perceiving in himself that power had gone out from him, immediately turned about in the crowd and said, 'Who touched my garments?'" (v. 30). The disciples looked around, confused. Many people had touched Jesus as they all pressed in on Him. But the woman came forward, fell at His feet, and told Him the whole truth. We assume when Mark writes "the whole truth" that this woman told Christ about the doctors, about the abuse, about losing all her money, about losing her connections to her family and community. We can imagine her saying, "I went here and there. I saw this doctor and that one. And finally I was without options. So I risked what little I had left to touch you."

And Jesus said to her, "Daughter, your faith has made you well; go in peace, and be healed of your disease" (v. 34).

❓ What did Jesus say made her well?

Jesus said it was her faith! Her faith encouraged her to not give up. Her faith pushed her through that crowd. Her faith gave her the strength to reach out and touch Jesus' robe. And her faith also made her brave enough to come forward when He looked for her in the crowd. Her faith in Him brought relief.

Your Faith Has Made You Well

It's interesting to note what Jesus commended in this woman. It wasn't her steadfastness. It wasn't her determination. It wasn't her willingness to elbow herself through the crowd. It was her faith.

When we have meetings about James, Sandra brings a binder full of information. Copies of therapy evaluations, results of blood tests, a list of medicines and supplements, his IEP, and more. It is obvious to others we are serious about helping him thrive. We want him to reach his potential. We take our care for him seriously. Like this woman, we have seen many doctors and therapists and have spent lots of money. Some of these doctors have helped and others haven't. But we continue to have faith.

What is our faith in? The medical community? The most recent study? The newest therapy trend? To a degree, yes. Or we wouldn't keep going there for answers. Hebrews 11:1 says, "Now faith is the assurance of things hoped for, the conviction of things not seen." We hope for James to feel better. We can't see it, but we hope for it. But ultimately, our hope is in Christ.

Author and pastor John Piper said, "The deepest need that you and I have in weakness and adversity is not quick relief, but the well-grounded confidence that what is happening to us is part of the greatest purpose of God in the universe—the glorification of the grace and power of his Son—the grace and power that bore him to the cross and kept him there until the work of love was done."[v]

We need faith. Faith that His purpose and will for our lives and the lives of our children will be fulfilled. Faith that when doctors, therapists, teachers, and even friends and family members fail us, He never will.

❓ Do you agree with John Piper, that your deepest need is not quick relief but confidence in God's plan? How does that change your perspective on searching for

solutions and bring you comfort if that
search ends with no clear solution?

Learning from the Faithful

The woman with the issue of blood is one of
many faithful people we read about in the Bible.
Hebrews chapter 11 lists many of their stories.
Abel, Enoch, Noah, Abraham, Sarah, Isaac,
Jacob, Joseph, Moses, the Israelites, and Rahab
are all recognized for their faith. The chapter
goes on to list more. Did all their situations work
out in what we would consider the best way?
There were healings, resurrections, and needs
met. But there was also mocking, flogging,
suffering, and killing. Verse 39 says, "And all
these, though commended through their faith,
did not receive what was promised, since God
had provided something better for us, that apart
from us they should not be made perfect."

We don't only have faith when we feel
God is being faithful to us by giving us what we
want. We have faith in Him, not in His actions or
inactions. As Pete Wilson writes, "We must
decide if we are going to put our faith in what
God does or in who God is."[vi]

The Apostle John could have been talking about anyone on the list in Hebrews 11 when he wrote, "For everyone who has been born of God overcomes the world. And this is the victory that has overcome the world — our faith" (1 John 5:4). They didn't all have victory over pain or suffering. They did have victory over this world.

Because we have faith in God, we can learn from the examples of those in the faith hall of fame of Hebrews 11. And we take seriously the admonition that follows in chapter 12, "[L]et us run with endurance the race that is set before us, looking to Jesus, the founder and perfecter of our faith" (12:1b–2a). Looking to Jesus — isn't that what the woman subject to bleeding did? She looked to Him, moved toward Him, and stayed in His presence. We can do the same. We can place our faith in Him. We may have to do it ten times a day, but we can do it. Let us run with endurance, with faith in our Savior who founded and continues to perfect our faith.

Chapter Three
The Purpose of Disability

In 2007, we walked across the stage at our seminary graduation. Sandra was pregnant at the time and whispered to our sweet baby James, "This chapel is filled with professors, authors, preachers, teachers, and missionaries. These are the world changers, baby, and you're going to be one too."

When we got his autism diagnosis, our dreams for him changed. Could he still be a world changer?

Last spring Lee stood at a booth for our church at our community's autism walk. Over two thousand people walked by the booth and saw our church's name. Some stopped and asked why a church would be at the walk. We were there to share the good news of God's love and tell the families our church is a safe place for them and their special-needs children.

One of the families who stopped at our booth that day has started visiting our church. Lee talked to the mom and she said, "We had decided we wanted to start taking the kids to church but were nervous. When you said your church had a special-needs ministry we were interested. But when you said you have a son with autism and that your church loves him, we knew it could be the church home for us."

Our church wouldn't have a special-needs ministry if it weren't for James. He was the catalyst for the ministry to start. We wouldn't host respite nights, have a special-needs Vacation Bible School class, or have buddies for special-needs kids in Sunday school and the service.

We didn't start the ministry, but James did. Church members saw there was a need and met the need. It started with James, but it hasn't ended with him. Families are being reached through the ministry. They are hearing the gospel. They are experiencing God's love. And ultimately, their worlds are changing.

When we think back to our dreams for James to be a world changer, we're amazed by how God has made that happen. What we saw as a weakness, God used as a strength. What we thought was the end was just the beginning.

? When you got your child's diagnosis, how did your dreams for him change? Was that process hard for you? Can you look back at it with confidence in God's plan, or are you still wondering what God may be up to?

Who Sinned?

God has a purpose for each of our children. We don't have to guess what it is. In John chapter 9, we can read about it in black and white (and red, if Jesus' words are red in your version).

In John 8, Jesus had said to His disciples, "I am the light of the world. Whoever follows me will not walk in darkness, but will have the light of life" (v. 12). Jesus illustrated that teaching when He and His disciples encountered a man who was blind from birth. That man had lived a life of darkness. How would Jesus show His disciples and this man what it meant to truly be the light of the world?

As John 9 opens, Jesus and his disciples were walking and passed a man blind from birth, and the verse says Jesus saw him. Jesus noticed him. I'm sure you have experienced situations out in public when people see your special-needs child. When they notice him or her. Sometimes it's positive, sometimes it's negative.

? Think about a time someone noticed the differences in your child. Was it a positive or negative experience for you and your family?

Sandra's sister Syble has Down syndrome, so when her family goes out to eat or out anywhere, people notice them. Sometimes they stare. Sometimes they smile. Sometimes they just look away. Young children may ask questions or point. It becomes so expected we don't even notice it anymore. But our son James has autism, which can't really be seen. Usually, it's heard. If we go to the grocery store and he screeches, people look. If we're at the park and he jumps and flaps, people notice. Depending on how loud he is or where we are, we sometimes get dirty looks or exasperated sighs in our direction. We've even gotten a few questions. When Jesus and His disciples passed this man with a disability, the disciples had a question.

"Rabbi, who sinned, this man or his parents, that he was born blind?" (John 9:2).

What's going on here, Jesus? Why is there suffering? Why do we have to see it every day? Why do we have to walk by it? Hear it cry out? Respond to it by either meeting the need or walking away? What is the cause of all this?

We assume they are still close enough for the man to hear this question. In verse six Jesus touches him, so they likely have this conversation just a few feet away. The blind man may have had the same question. If he had known who this man was who passed by and saw him that day, he probably would have asked Him the same questions. "Why Rabbi? Why God? Why this darkness? Why me?"

In Exodus 4:11 the Lord asked Moses, "Who has made man's mouth? Who makes him mute, or deaf, or seeing, or blind? Is it not I, the Lord?" It is the Lord. And because it is the Lord who allows these disabilities, these differences, He must have a reason.

Jesus doesn't answer with the *cause* of disability, He answers with the *purpose* of disability.

"It was not that this man sinned, or his parents, but that the works of God might be displayed in him" (John 9:3).

It's no one's fault. His parents aren't being punished and neither is he. Many parents of special-needs children struggle with this. We wonder if it's our fault. If we're being punished by God for something we did or didn't do. Nancy Guthrie lost two children soon after their births. She writes, "There is a purpose for this suffering. Like many people who experience difficulty, I immediately made the assumption that my suffering was my fault, that all my sins had caught up with me and I was finally getting what I deserved."[vii] And Amy Julia Becker, who wrote *Good and Perfect Gift* about the birth of her daughter with Down syndrome, says, "Penny is neither a rebuke nor a reward. She is a child, not a product of sin or of biological happenstance or of any lesson we needed to learn. No. This happened that the glory of God might be revealed."[viii]

❓ In Sandra's first book, *Speechless: Finding God's Grace in My Son's Autism*, she writes honestly about the struggles she had accepting James's diagnosis. Did you (or do you) also struggle with feelings of being punished or that you deserve to suffer (or see your child suffer)?

How Disabilities Point Us to God

The very first Westminster Catechism gets right to the point:
Question 1: What is the chief end of man?
Answer: Man's chief end is to glorify God, and to enjoy him forever.

This man was born blind so his life would display the power of God. So his blindness would display the power of God. So his begging would display the power of God. So the very corner he sat on would display the power of God.

We must ask, how does his life display the power of God? Well, in this specific situation, Jesus healed him from his blindness. "Then he anointed the man's eyes with the mud and said to him, 'Go wash in the pool of Siloam' (which means Sent). So he went and washed and came back seeing" (vv. 6b–7). He took the man from a life of darkness to a life of light.

Word of the miracle Jesus performed spread throughout the town. "The neighbors and those who had seen him before as a beggar were saying, 'Is this not the man who used to sit and beg?' Some said, 'It is he.' Others said, 'No, but he is like him.' He kept saying, 'I am the man.'" (vv. 8–9). They take the previously blind man to the Pharisees to see what they think. They were confused about what happened to this man. Some doubted the man's story. Those who did believe doubted the healing was from God because Jesus performed the miracle on the Sabbath.

In verse 18 we read the Jews asked the man's parents if he had truly been born blind. If anyone is going to know the truth about this man's disabilities, it's his parents. We keep three-ring binders full of information from each year since James's diagnosis. If someone were to knock on our door and ask for proof of his disability, we could pull the binders off the shelf and show them receipts for weekly occupational therapy, copies of his IEPs, the VB-MAPP his behavioral therapist uses to track his progress, a record of doctors visits, and page after page of insurance claims. Need proof of disability? We've got it. Need proof of God working in his life? We've got that too.

But these parents were scared. Verse 22 says the Jews had already said anyone who confessed Jesus to be Christ would be put out of the synagogue, and therefore cut off from the center of life for Jews in that day. They answered, "We know that he is our son and that he was born blind. But how he now sees we do not know, nor do we know who opened his eyes. Ask him: he is of age. He will speak for himself" (v. 20).

So for a second time they ask the previously blind man what happened to him and he told them—again. He said to them, "Never since the world began has it been heard that anyone opened the eyes of a man born blind. If this man were not from God, he could do nothing" (vv. 32–33). God had a purpose in this man's blindness and also in his healing. Jesus' compassion and mercy were on full display in this man's life. The Jews couldn't explain away this man's miracle, so they cast him out. This blind man had been an outcast before, but he was at least still part of the community. Though he was a beggar, he at least had some where to sit and beg. Now, he had his sight, but he had no home.

? Sometimes our situations seem to get worse before they get better. With autism, a breakthrough in one area often means regression in another. Can you think of an example from your life when things seemed to get worse?

At the end of chapter 9 it says Jesus heard about what happened to him and sought him out. They talked about what happened. "Jesus heard that they had cast him out, and having found him he said, 'Do you believe in the Son of Man?' He answered, 'And who is he sir, that I may believe in him?' Jesus said to him, 'You have seen him, and it is he who is speaking to you.' He said, 'Lord, I believe,' and he worshipped him" (vv. 35–37).

This had to be an exhausting day for this man. That morning he sat on the road as he had probably done for months, perhaps years, to beg for help. A group of men came up and asked their teacher about his condition. That teacher healed him, but the religious leaders harassed him and even questioned his parents. He was excommunicated and needed help again. But through this conversation with Jesus, we see at the end of the day, he believed and worshiped. Isn't that what we want said of us at the end of a long day? That we believed and worshipped? Even when stared at or questioned. Even when our children make progress in one area and then regress in another.

When There Is No Miracle

Nancy Guthrie writes, "While the miracles Jesus performed reveal his love and compassion for hurting people, the greater purpose of each miracle was to draw people into a deeper spiritual reality, a greater understanding of him that will give us the life we're so desperate for."[ix] What do we do when the result isn't healing? Do we stop believing and withhold worship?

That's not what Paul did. He had a disability, a thorn in the flesh as he called it. In 2 Corinthians 9, Paul cried out for healing. He begged for mercy. "Three times I pleaded with the Lord about this, that it should leave me. But he said to me, 'My grace is sufficient for you, for my power is made perfect in weakness'" (vv. 8–9).

J. I. Packer states, "But supernatural healings in equal abundance to those worked in the days of Jesus' flesh may not be his will today. The question concerns not his power but his purpose. We cannot guarantee that because he healed the sick brought to him then, he will do the same now."[x] The purpose of disability in the life of the man born blind was to show God's might. The purpose of disability in the life of Paul was to show God's power.

❓ Do you struggle trusting God's plan when you can't see evidence of His power? Have you ever felt like if you had more faith your child might be healed? How does Paul's situation bring you comfort?

Our children, no matter their disabilities, will fulfill the purposes God has for them. This chapter in John makes that clear. We believe God is already doing that in James's life through the special-needs ministry that has started at our church. We believe it when James's disability opens the door for us to talk to his teacher about the hope we have in Christ. We believe it when we get an email from someone who read our first book, *Speechless: Finding God's Grace in My Son's Autism,* and found grace from God through our story of His grace. "God's primary purpose in the here and now is not to rid us of sickness and pain but to purify us and empower us to place all our hopes in his promises, trusting that one day they will become the reality we will know fully and enjoy forever."[xi]

"Those who sow in tears shall reap with shouts of joy!" says Psalm 126:5. The man born blind testifies to this truth. So does Paul. And so do we.

Chapter 4
When Others Don't Get It

Sandra can remember the very first time she heard someone make fun of those with disabilities. In second grade on the playground, two friends made moaning noises, hit themselves in the chests, and said, "Look, I'm retarded." Since Sandra's sister has Downs, she knew the word "retarded" but had never heard it as an insult before, as a joke. She went home and cried to her mom, asking why people would make fun of people with disabilities. Decades later, we're still hearing "retarded" as an insult and jokes about the short bus, special ed classes, and other comments that show some people just don't get it.

What's even harder than hearing jokes like these on TV or on the playground is when our friends or family members show they just don't get it. We often talk to parents of kids with autism who tell us their family members claim they just aren't strict enough. If they would just make their child sit still, or eat that food, or make eye contact, then he or she would be normal. Others have teachers who continue to give their children snacks with ingredients their children are allergic or sensitive to, like gluten or food dyes. And some parents have to call ahead to make sure there is handicap parking available and convenient ramps so their family can attend events other families just hop in the car and drive off to. The struggle for us is how to react in situations like these, when people just don't get it.

Throughout the gospels, the disciples just didn't always get it. Jesus told them stories they didn't understand. He did miracles they didn't get. He even died just as He said He would, and they still weren't sure what happened. We can learn from how Jesus treated His closest friends, even when (especially when!) they were clueless. He was tempted to react with frustration. Hebrews 4:15 says Jesus "in every respect has been tempted as we are, yet without sin." And in chapter 12, it also says, "let us run with endurance the race that is set before us, looking to Jesus, the founder and perfecter of our faith" (1b–2a). Because Christ was tempted as we are, and because He is the founder and perfecter of our faith, we can look to His example. We can learn from the ways He responded.

❓ Some stories of when friends or family just didn't get it are hurtful and some are humorous. Do you have a story to share of either instance? How did you respond?

The Disciples Just Didn't Get It

Twice in the book of Matthew we see examples of Christ's patience with the disciples. First, in chapter 19, a man approached Jesus and asked how he could have eternal life. Jesus spoke of the commandments. The man replied, "All these I have kept. What do I still lack?" And Jesus told him he must sell all he had to give to the poor and follow Him. The man we know as the rich young ruler walked away sad, because he had great possessions. Jesus turned to His disciples to make this a teaching moment for them. "Truly I say to you, only with difficulty will a rich person enter the kingdom of heaven. Again I tell you, it is easier for a camel to go through the eye of a needle than for a rich person to enter the kingdom of God" (vv. 23–24). Verse 25 says when the disciples heard this, they were astonished. They didn't get it. If this were true, they wondered who could be saved. What did Jesus do? He looked at them and said, "With man this is impossible, but with God all things are possible." Peter voiced the disciples' concerns: "See, we have left everything and followed you. What then will we have?" Jesus patiently answered again, giving further details and application.

In the next chapter in Matthew, they don't get it again. James and John's mom had a request for Jesus, "Say that these two sons of mine are to sit, one at your right hand and one at your left, in your kingdom" (20:21b). Since she walked up to Jesus with her sons, some speculate they may have even put her up to asking. When Lee coached basketball, he often had parents make requests for their boys, especially for more playing time. When Sandra was a teacher, parents of her students asked for special privileges or for their children to be allowed to bend the rules.

Jesus had told the disciples at the end of chapter 19 that the first would be last, but this request makes it clear they didn't get it. So He taught them the lesson again. "You know that the rulers of the Gentiles lord it over them, and their great ones exercise authority over them. It shall not be so among you. But whoever would be great among you must be your servant, and whoever would be first among you must be your slave, even as the Son of Man came not to be served but to serve, and to give his life as a ransom for many" (vv. 25–28).

Surly the disciples got it then, right? There's no reward for pride in God's economy. No extra points for stepping over others to get first place. No, according to the book of Mark, Jesus had to remind them at least one more time. "And they came to Capernaum. And when he was in the house he asked them, 'What were you discussing on the way?' But they kept silent, for on the way they had argued with one another about who was the greatest" (Mark 9:33–34). Again they argued. Again they jockeyed for the highest position, for the most recognition. Again, Jesus responded with patience. The next verse says He sat down and called them to Himself, "If anyone would be first, he must be last of all and servant of all" (v. 35).

What Did Jesus Do?

Jesus' example is one of patience and keeping the peace. He was never argumentative or disrespectful. Never rolled His eyes or sighed with exasperation. Never turned red in the face or stomped his foot with His hands on His hips. He taught the same lesson again and again. He made eye contact and gathered his friends close to Himself. He used different illustrations. His goal was not to be right, but that they would understand. This wasn't a battle to win, it was an opportunity to teach.

As we communicate with others who may not understand our children's disabilities and what caring for them requires from us, we also need to realize this isn't a battle to win. This isn't about who has the hardest life, or goes to more doctors' appointments, or who will never have an empty nest. Just like there was no real competition with the disciples, there's no real competition with us.

❓ What stands out to you about how Jesus responded to the disciples? His patience? His calmness? His willingness to explain lessons again and again? How can you learn from His example and apply His characteristics to a situation you're in right now?

Forgiving Each Other

Making fun of people with disabilities doesn't just happen in second grade on the playground. We have all had run-ins with people who don't understand their words hurt.

The special-needs community recently reacted to lyrics from the song "Jodeci Freestyle" from hip-hop artists Drake and J.Cole. They used autistic and retarded as insults in their song. Both have since come out with apologies, but thousands of young people are singing along to the lyrics, thinking nothing of the people they are insulting.

"End the R-Word" is now a national campaign, but Sandra feels like she's been a part of it since she first heard it used. Her friends in high school knew her sister Syble, so she didn't hear it often from them. But as she went off to college, she felt like she needed to speak up when people used it as an insult. She even spoke to the youth minister at her church after he used it in a Wednesday night sermon to the youth group.

We hear jokes about people having to ride the short bus or special ed kids ("sp ed" as we've heard them called). At a recent night with friends, Sandra listened to two friends joke that one of their husbands was "so special, like sp ed."

Jesus understood being made fun of by people who didn't really understand what they were saying. Some of His last words from the cross were, "Father, forgive them, for they know not what they do" (Luke 23:34). If we dwell on all the insults and not-funny jokes, we can become angry and bitter. Like Christ, we need to extend forgiveness. Colossians 3:13 says "as the Lord has forgiven you, so you also must forgive." Don't carry around anger or resentment. If you have the opportunity to educate others, do so. But when you can't, pray for the other person to realize how hurtful his or her words are, and then forgive. You don't have enough energy to hold a grudge over someone who was just trying to be funny.

❓ Have you been hurt by someone else's careless words? Are you still holding onto anger or have you forgiven that person?

Our Goal Is Peace

We need to have patience with others. We may not always get it in return, but we are Christ-followers. We are different. When we have reasons to get angry and don't, others notice. God notices. Of course, we stand up for our rights and the rights of our children, but we remember to display the fruit of the Spirit (Gal. 5:22–23: love, joy, peace, patience, kindness, goodness, faithfulness, gentleness, and self-control). We know we will give an account to God for our actions and words. All we can do is our best and ask the Holy Spirit to work through us.

Romans 12:16a and 18 say, "Live in harmony with one another. If possible, so far as it depends on you, live peaceably with all." This isn't easy when you feel like the world is against you. We have to remind ourselves of this especially when we travel on airplanes. It's impossible to keep James still and quiet for the more than three-hour plane ride it takes to get us to Houston to see Sandra's family. We've dealt with dirty looks, rolling eyes, and lots of exasperated sighs. We heard of one family with a son with autism who passed out cookies and earplugs to everyone sitting around their family on the plane, with a note that explained what autism was and thanked them for their patience. Sounds like a good idea!

Situations with family members and friends are even harder than with strangers. One family we know really struggles with the actions and attitudes of the husband's parents. They pay attention to the typical child in the family and ignore their grandson who has cerebral palsy. They even buy gifts for the typical grandchild only, saying their special-needs grandson doesn't know the difference. Even if he doesn't know, the parents know. The typical sibling knows. And it hurts them all.

We feel hurt by not only friends and family members, but sometimes by the church. We recently read *Leading a Special Needs Ministry* by Amy Fenton Lee. In it, Amy interviewed many mothers who were hurt by their churches during time in their lives they got their children's diagnoses. Many told her of how a difficult time was made worse by neglect or negative reactions. Amy writes, "My desire was for the next wave of mothers to tell stories of comfort, connection, and renewal when they recounted their church experiences. Perhaps the people of the church could provide a spiritual oasis in the midst of an otherwise chaotic life."[xii] Amy's advice tells pastors and church members what to expect and how to act as they minister to families through these situations. And we can help too by being available to walk with others who are just starting on their special needs journeys.

? Think honestly about your feelings toward friends and family who you feel may have let you down. If there is bitterness or resentment in your heart, pray and ask God to heal those wounds. This has been a process for us and we don't want to gloss over the pain you feel others have caused or contributed to. If you have put up walls, afraid of being hurt again, ask God to help you learn to trust.

Jesus was misunderstood by friends, those who mocked Him, and even family members. He had brothers who didn't believe in Him (John 7:5). But since His brother James went on to write the book of James, we know he eventually did believe Jesus was who He said He was. His family finally got it and yours may too. Turn the situation over to God in prayer. Believe that He understands and has compassion for you. Continue to walk worthy of the gospel message and pray you can be a light to others.

Chapter 5
Better Together

Story from Katie- Community Leader for an On-Line Special-Need Support Group

We have three kids. They are fabulous. Our oldest had been in therapy for childhood apraxia of speech and motor delays since she was eighteen-months. The last four years — Ry is now six — have truly been a blur of appointments, pregnancies, and late-night feedings. When I finally surfaced a year ago, I found myself on the fringes of friendships and without the real time to make meaningful connections. I was alone. And not the healthy, re-charge, rest kind of alone. I was specifically without other women who knew what my life — especially life as a mom of a special-needs kid — looked like on a daily basis.

I don't remember how I found it, but I saw that DaySpring's (in)courage ministry was looking to start some online communities, and they were taking applications for groups leaders. They had all of their intended groups listed: homeschooling moms, Bible study moms, empty-nesters ... all the usual life stages. But no special-needs moms. And so I threw in my application, which shocked both me and God, I'm certain.

A year later, our little group that is supposed to hover around fifty is huge and happy at one hundred sixty-five, with a core group of moms who have become dear online friends … including our own Sandra Peoples. We all have different stories and different questions and different churches … but we all have kids with special needs. We all know. It takes little more than a jumbled prayer-request or an alphabet soup diagnosis to get our moms nodding their heads and jumping in to pray, to advise, to laugh, to cry. They get it.

It was clear from the immediate response and the unlikely online bonds that quickly formed that many of us had been waiting for this for a long time. An easy, no-pressure, no expectations, no time-commitments outlet. No waiting rooms, no forms to fill out—just faith-based community centered on daily life and special-needs kids.

I am blessed to hold the door open for these saints to enter into community. I am only the leader because I needed this group the most. Thank God, literally, He took me to the edges of my comfort zone yet again and showed me I am not alone.

? Katie says she lost track of friends when she was focused on her family's needs. Can you relate? How have your friendships changed since your child's diagnosis?

? Katie found community by being willing to be used by God to lead it. How has God used you to minister to others in the special-needs world?

Friends Find a Way

In Mark 2, we are introduced to a paralytic man. The beginning of the story isn't really about him, it's about his four friends. They are the heroes in these verses.

Jesus was teaching in Capernaum. Many were gathered in the home where He was preaching the word. So many, verse 2 says, there was no more room, not even at the door. But the four men wanted to get their paralytic friend to Jesus. They knew with Jesus there was healing. There was comfort. There was peace. There was everything their paralytic friend needed, and since he couldn't get to Jesus on his own, they stepped up to help.

"And when they could not get near him because of the crowd, they removed the roof above him, and when they had made an opening, they let down the bed on which the paralytic lay" (v 4). Jesus couldn't help but notice a man on a mat coming down through the roof. And what was his response? "And when Jesus saw their faith, he said to the paralytic, 'My son, your sins are forgiven.'" It wasn't the faith of the paralytic man that Jesus rewarded. In the chapter before, Jesus healed a leper because he begged of Him, "If you will, you can make me clean" (Mark 1:40). But this man didn't speak a word. He didn't move a muscle. It was the faith of his friends that made the difference.

The weariness we feel as special-needs parents is heavier than any weariness we have felt before. Deeper than staying up too late in college and rolling out of bed for an early class. Stronger than multiple feedings during the early nights of having an infant. This weariness doesn't let up. It isn't cured with a thirty-minute power nap or a pint of ice cream. Your body and soul adjust to this new normal and you get into a routine that alleviates the weariness, but it never fully lifts.

That must have been how the paralytic man felt. We aren't told how many years he had been a paralytic. We don't know what he was able to do for himself. We know he was so weary that he was being carried through the streets of Capernaum to catch the attention of a man who had the reputation of healing others. If there was any truth to this rumor, this man's friends were willing to do the heavy lifting to find out. They took the steps toward Jesus. They pulled the man up on the roof with his mat. They cut through crowds and the ceiling to make a way for their friend. They had faith that, with their help, their weary friend would find what he needed most.

What was the result of their faith? "… he said to the paralytic—'I say to you, rise, pick up your bed, and go home.' And he rose and immediately picked up his bed and went out before them all, so that they were all amazed and glorified God, saying, 'We never saw anything like this!'" (2:10–12). The man's sins were forgiven, he was healed and able to walk, and the crowd glorified God. The paralytic man didn't even have to get out of bed that day. His friends picked him up, bed and all, and brought him to the miracle. Their faith was rewarded and God was glorified.

? We see the results of the friends' faith. What did it cause the crowd to do in verse 12?

Strength When You Have None

In Exodus we read about another man who was fighting a hard battle and needed help from others. Moses had led the Israelites out of Egypt and through the Red Sea. They weren't a happy bunch though, constantly grumbling and demanding more from Moses. "Why did you bring us out of Egypt to kill us?" they asked when hungry or thirsty. We've been on some pretty long road trips and know what it's like to travel when we're all hungry or thirsty. Multiply that by the up to one million people we believe Moses was leading on this off-road trip, and you can imagine that if he could have pulled that car over and left them at the next rest stop, he would have.

Not only were his own people grumbling against him, but Amalek came to fight with Israel. Moses appointed Joshua and his men to go into battle. Moses stood on the top of a hill to watch, with the staff of God in his hand. Exodus 17:11 says, "Whenever Moses held up his hand, Israel prevailed, and whenever he lowered his hand, Amalek prevailed." Moses was already weary. And now he had the key to the battle in his hands—his very tired hands.

We've all felt that burden of responsibility, haven't we? Thinking if we don't make that phone call, or drive to that therapy session, or research that new medicine it would never happen. The battle would be lost.

As the battle dragged on, Moses needed help. "But Moses' hands grew weary, so they took a stone and put it under him, and he sat on it, while Aaron and Hur held up his hands, one on one side, and the other on the other side. So his hands were steady until the going down of the sun" (Exod. 17:12). Moses still did his job—he held up the staff—but he did it with help. He drew on the strength of others to accomplish the goal.

> ❓ Who helps you when you are weary? A spouse or other family member? A therapist or teacher? A friend? Give thanks to God for that person today.

Building Community

We all need help at times. The days surrounding your child's diagnosis can feel like the loneliest days you've ever experienced. Like Naomi, you may want to walk up to people and say, "Do not call me Naomi; call me Mara, for the Almighty has dealt very bitterly with me. I went away full, and the Lord has brought me back empty" (Ruth 1:20–21). The name "Naomi" means pleasant and the name "Mara" means bitter.

But let's give Naomi credit—she didn't lie about her pain. She didn't pretend everything was okay when it really wasn't. She was honest enough and trusted her faith community enough to tell the truth. Martin Lloyd-Jones writes, "It is so easy to live an artificial and a superficial life and to persuade ourselves that we really are what we would like to be. But in a time of trial and crisis, the natural, the real, and true come into view."[xiii]

This isn't always easy. If you are the do-it-yourself type, it will be hard to be vulnerable. If you like to keep things to yourself, it will be hard to open up. We felt extra pressure because we are in ministry. The pastor and pastor's wife are supposed to have it together, right? We're supposed to be strong for others. We're supposed to comfort the mourning. We're supposed to give good advice. And to be completely honest, we were still strong, offered comfort, and gave advice, even in the midst of our personal pain and confusion. People still sat in Lee's office and cried over situations we felt were much less traumatic than what we were going through. Early in our special-needs journey, we didn't feel like anyone was ministering to us the way we ministered to others.

An autism diagnosis isn't like a cancer diagnosis. People who haven't experienced it don't realize there is a grieving process. Friends didn't ask how we were doing. No one brought meals by. Church members didn't offer to help Lee with his ministry load so he could focus on our family situation. We suffered mostly in silence. But as God healed us, He also worked in the lives of those around us. We gave them time and space to process the changes in our family and they are now a great support system for us.

Dustin Shramek writes, "We don't love others in the midst of this kind of pain by pretending that it isn't all that bad or by trying to quickly fix it with some pat theological answer. We love them by first weeping with them. It is when we enter into their pain and are ourselves changed by it that we can speak the truth in love. When their pain becomes our pain (as Paul said, 'If one member suffers, all suffer together' [1 Cor. 12:26]), we are able to give the encouragement of the Scriptures."[xiv]

We are no longer the only family in our church who has a child with special needs. As we mentioned in a previous chapter, the love our church has shown to us has grown to include others. We've connected with families through James's school. We have a very active autism support group in our county that has meetings and a variety of activities throughout the month. A community of five hundred fans has been built on Facebook around Sandra's first book, *Speechless*. Sandra writes for the special-needs parents' website, Not Alone, where readers share prayer requests every day and the writers lift them up.

When we couldn't find community, we built it. As C. S. Lewis famously said, "Friendship … is born at the moment when one man says to another, 'What! You too? I thought that no one but myself … '"[xv] Sandra spoke to other moms in the waiting room during James's occupational and speech therapy sessions. Lee was intentional about connecting with special-needs families who attend our church's respite nights. We even learned our favorite checker at the grocery store has a granddaughter with autism! We prayed for opportunities to connect and God brought people into our lives.

> ❓ How have you connected with other families who have children with special needs? If you haven't connected yet, how has this chapter encouraged you to do so?

You Need Friends

You need friends who will carry you. Who will lift up your weary arms. Who you can be honest with. Pray for these friends. Reach out and be this type of friend to others. God knows how important community is. That's why He set up the institution of the church. That's why believers are referred to as brothers and sisters in the New Testament. God will provide community for you.

Chapter 6
Facing Our Fears

When James gets home from school each day, we ask how it went. He doesn't reply. He can't tell us if it was a good day or a bad day. He can't tell us what he ate or what he learned. He isn't verbal enough to tell us much. We worry about that. We worry that he will be the victim of abuse or bullying. We worry about elopement. According to a study by The Interactive Autism Network, half of parents of children with autism report their children with autism elope. 50% of these families say their children were gone long enough to cause them worry. The study also showed:

- Wandering was ranked among the most stressful ASD behaviors by 58% of parents of elopers

- 62% of families of children who elope were prevented from attending/enjoying activities outside the home due to fear of wandering

- 40% of parents had suffered sleep disruption due to fear of elopement

- Children with ASD are eight times more likely to elope between the ages of 7 and 10 than their typically-developing sibling

Our children don't really elope, or run away, on purpose. They are unaware of the danger they put themselves in. In fact, the study also showed the top five reasons parents believed their children eloped:

- Enjoys exploring (54%)

- Heads for a favorite place (36%)

- Escapes demands/anxieties (33%)

- Pursues special topic (31%)

- Escapes sensory discomfort (27%)[xvi]

In addition to fearing elopement, we also fear James will be abused. Good friends of ours had their adult son with autism in a full-time care facility. They trusted the people there to care for their son. But when they realized he was being abused, that trust was broken and he returned home.

These worries are real. They happen to families every day. But we can't let the fear paralyze us. We have to live and love in faith.

R. C. Sproul writes, "God, in his providence, has the power and the will to work all things together for good for his people. This does not mean that everything that happens to us is, in itself, good. Really bad things do happen to us. But they are only proximately bad; they are never ultimately bad. That is, they are bad only in the short (proximate) term, never in the long term. Because of the triumph of God's goodness in all things, he is able to bring good for us out of the bad. He turns our tragedies into supreme blessings."[xvii]

> **?** What are some of your biggest fears for your child?

Teacher, Do You Not Care?

In Mark 4, the disciples were on a boat in a storm. Verse 37 says, "And a great windstorm arose, and the waves were breaking into the boat, so that the boat was already filling." This time, Jesus was on the boat with them. Verse 38 says he was asleep on a cushion. The disciples woke Him and said, "Teacher, do you not care that we are perishing?"

We have felt that way before—like we're in a storm and Jesus doesn't seem to care. We don't feel His presence. We worry for our lives and for our children. We can even convince ourselves He doesn't know what's going on in our lives. That He's curled up on a pillow while our entire world falls apart around us. But, those feelings aren't true. Psalm 121:4 tells us God does not slumber nor sleep. 1 Peter 5:7 says we are to cast our anxieties on Him because He cares for us. When we hear the whisper in our ears that God doesn't care, we must fight back with the truth. Philip Yancey writes, "God is not deaf. God is as grieved by the world's trauma as you are. His only son died here. But God has promised to set things right."[xviii]

Back in our scene in Mark 4, Jesus woke up and calmed the storm by saying, "Peace! Be still!" Then He turned to His disciples and asked, "Why are you so afraid? Have you no faith?" (v. 40). The weapon against fear is faith.

? What can we have faith in based on the following verses?

Jeremiah 29:11

Isaiah 52:12

Philippians 4:19

John 3:16

When we have this faith, we do not fear. "There is no fear in love, but perfect love casts out fear" (1 John 4:19a). John Calvin wrote, "When the light of Divine Providence has illuminated the believer's soul, he is relieved and set free, not only from the extreme fear and anxiety which formerly oppressed him, but from all care."[xix]

> **?** Some people tend to worry more than others because of their personality types and even spiritual giftedness. Lee tends to worry about more than Sandra does. Are you a worrier? What has helped you stop worrying (or at least worry less)?

God Will Provide

A few months after James's diagnosis, we went to our first local autism support group meeting. The speaker worked for the Social Security Administration and had two sons on the spectrum. He went over what financial help families like ours could expect when our children get older. He also talked about how we could provide for our children's care even after our deaths. Because Sandra's parents were working on their wills at the time, we were having conversations about her sister Syble's future. We knew there couldn't be any property or accounts in Syble's name. Everything she needed had to be put in a trust fund with a guardianship.

We looked around the room at that meeting and saw worry on the other parents' faces. What would happen to their special-needs children? What burden would they pass on to their typical children? How could they possibly prepare for all the what-ifs?

One of the most pressing worries of parents with special-needs children is what will happen to them when we pass away or are no longer able to care for them. It can keep us up at night, tossing and turning, thinking and praying.

In the last chapter of 1 Samuel, we read about Saul's death, and the deaths of his sons Jonathan, Abinidab, and Malchishua. David had already been anointed king by Samuel, but had been on the run from Saul, who was jealous and wanted him dead. In 1 Samuel 18:8, Saul says, "They ascribe to David ten thousands, and to me they have ascribed thousands, and what more can he have but the kingdom?" The next verse says from that day on, Saul eyed David. But David and Saul's son Jonathan became friends. Jonathan warned David when his father was going to attack and said to him, "Go in peace, because we have sworn both of us in the name of the Lord, saying, 'The Lord shall be between me and you, and between my offspring and your offspring, forever'" (1 Sam. 20:42). After Jonathan's death, would David remember their vow?

In 2 Samuel 9 we find out. David asked, "Is there anyone left in the house of Saul, that I may show him kindness for Jonathan's sake?" (v. 1). A servant told David, "There is still a son of Jonathan; he is crippled in his feet." At the news of his father's death, Mephibosheth's nurse took him and fled. In her haste, he fell and became lame (2 Samuel 4:4). Jonathan's son was dependent on others for his care. David asked for Mephibosheth to be brought to him. Mephibosheth came before the king and fell on his face before him. David said, "Do not fear, for I will show you kindness for the sake of your father Jonathan, and I will restore to you all the land of Saul your father, and you shall eat at my table always" (v. 7). Verse 11 says, "So

Mephibosheth ate at David's table, like one of the king's sons."

God did not forget Mephibosheth. He didn't let David forget either. Mephibosheth probably felt like he was alone and forgotten until David found him, but he never was. Isaiah 50:10 says, "Let him who walks in darkness and has no light, trust in the name of the Lord and rely on his God." Even during the darkest times, we don't have to fear because we trust in Him.

An Illustration from Paula Simonson, a friend Sandra met online

I was mowing the yard in the early spring and felt a strong impression that I should throw a big birthday party for my son Sam. Sam would turn seven in July, but due to his delays and disabilities he did not have many friends in his peer group. The party I pictured would be at the park, with whole families we knew who cared about him. We would have a rainbow theme. I really felt like this was God's idea, but rainbows at a seven year old boy's party?

When the party day arrived, I frosted many cupcakes in six different colors and arranged them in the shape of a rainbow on a picnic table in the pavilion of our local park. We played fun games until supper time, when I called everyone in to thank them for loving Sam and to sing happy birthday to him. As we started singing, it began to rain—a hard, driving rain, coming down horizontally due to the strong winds. Everyone huddled in the middle of the open shelter.

Some people tried to eat, but the wind was so strong the colorful plates just flew away. Then at last it calmed some and the sun tried to break through. Then someone noticed it — the rainbow, perfectly curved over the cross on the steeple of the local church. At Sam's birthday party, God reminded us in a spectacular way that He was with us, saw our struggles, and cared about our son. The storm felt like a metaphor for his life. His medical problems often terrified us and made it difficult to live a normal life. Sometimes we just huddled down, trying to survive it all. But God knew, God saw, and God was present in the midst of the storm.

❓ What has God used to encourage you, like Paula was encouraged by the rainbow? A song? A book? A sermon?

The future is unknown, but we trust in God who sees from the beginning to the end. Corrie Ten Boom, who survived a concentration camp in World War II, recalled this story:

> When I was a little girl, I went to my father and said, "Daddy, I am afraid that I will never be strong enough to be a martyr for Jesus Christ."
>
> "Tell me," Father said, "when you take a train trip from Haarlem to Amsterdam, when do I give you the money for the ticket? Three weeks before?"
>
> "No, Daddy, you give me the money for the ticket just before we get on the train."
>
> "That is right," my father said, "and so it is with God's strength. Our wise Father in heaven knows when you are going to need things too. Today you do not need the strength to be a martyr; but as soon as you are called upon for the honor of facing death for Jesus, he will supply the strength you need—just in time."[xx]

❓ Can you relate to Corrie Ten Boom's story? Have you experienced God's provision, even in the midst of pain and trials? Share your story and remember God will provide again, just in time.

God knows what strength you will need. He knows the battles you will face. He knows the heartbreak you may feel. Psalm 34:4 says, "I sought the Lord, and he answered me and delivered me from all my fears." Seek Him today. Listen for His answer. Experience His deliverance. And fear not.

Chapter 7
Pressing On

We are just at the beginning of our journey as special-needs parents. James is in kindergarten this year. We have years of IEPs and therapists' appointments ahead of us, years of doctors and diets. But because Sandra has been in a special-needs family since the day she was born, we know firsthand some of the challenges that lie ahead. We know there will be times our routine will be smooth and even feel easy. We know there will be times we have to make big changes and serious decisions.

In this last chapter, we want to leave you with encouragement no matter where you are in the special-needs journey. More than advice, we want to give you the power of Scripture, because only God's Word is living and active (Hebrews 4:12). When you put this book on the shelf, it's the truth of Scripture that will still work in your heart, not our words.

Your Ministry

Acts 17:26 says God made from one man every nation. He determined when and where each person would live. We read in Psalm 139 that before you were even born, your days were written in His book. He has placed you where you are, at the time you are there, with a purpose. That purpose is your ministry. How do you know what that ministry is and how do you determine if you're successful at it?

In a sermon in Ephesus, Paul said, "I do not account my life of any value nor as precious to myself, if only I may finish my course and the ministry that I received from the Lord Jesus, to testify to the gospel of the grace of God" (Acts 20:24).

Even if you don't have an official ministry position like Lee does, you have a ministry. Like Paul, your goal is to testify of the gospel of the grace of God. It's easy to believe we are testifying of the gospel when we are at church or even meeting with friends, talking about the blessings God has given us. It's hard to feel like you are testifying of the gospel when you are changing diapers, pulling the wheelchair out of the van, or asking your child to repeat the word again and again because you just can't understand it. But that is your calling and your opportunity. You testify of His gospel and grace when you love and serve your child.

? How do we accomplish the ministry we received from the Lord? Let's look at the instruction in the following verses:

2 Peter 3:18

Galatians 5:22-25

1 John 4:19

We grow in godliness. We exhibit the fruit of the Spirit. We love as we have been loved. And what better way to take these actions than when we serve our children?

Your Cross to Bear or Sanctifying Sandpaper?

Some days it's hard to focus on our ministries because we're so overwhelmed by our burdens. But God often uses our burdens as ministry. Joni Erickson Tada, a quadriplegic, reminds us,

> Please know that when I take up my cross every day, I'm not talking about my wheelchair. My wheelchair is not my cross to bear. Neither is your cane or walker your cross. Neither is your dead-end job or your irksome in-laws. … My cross to bear is not my wheelchair; it is my attitude. … Any complaints, any grumblings, and disputings or murmurings, any anxieties, any worries, and

resentments or anything that hints of a raging torrent of bitterness — these are the things God calls me to die to daily. For when I do, I not only become like him in his death (that is, taking up my cross and dying to the sin that he died for on his cross), but the power of the resurrection puts to death any doubts, fears, grumblings, and disputings.[xxi]

The very things we believe to be heavy burdens are the tools God is using to sanctify us. Greg Lucas writes,

I often wonder what it would be like to be a normal dad, of a normal family, with a normal son. I sometimes imagine sitting through an entire church service or ball game or date with my wife without having to answer an urgent alarm activated by Jake. I would probably have more friends, more time, and more worldly accomplishments. I would definitely have more pride.

In exchange, there would be less opportunity to recognize the amazing grace that God displays each and every day through the disability of my son. It is this grace that humiliates my pride, humbles my soul, deepens my shallowness, and allows me to see what is most important in life.[xxii]

We have a term for circumstances or people in our lives God seems to be using to make us more like His Son (in pleasant and not so pleasant ways) — sanctifying sandpaper. Oh, it rubs! And often hurts. But we are becoming smoother. He is making us new creations (2 Cor. 5:17). Even though it isn't easy, "we do not lose heart. Though our outer nature is wasting away, our inner nature is being renewed day by day. For this slight momentary affliction is preparing for us an eternal weight of glory beyond all comparison, as we look not to the things that are seen but to the things that are unseen. For the things that are seen are transient, but the things that are unseen are eternal" (2 Cor 4:16–18).

? How has God used your child's disability to sanctify you? What areas of sin have been rubbed smooth because of your child's influence on your life?

Straining Toward the Goal

What we need as parents of children with special needs is strength for today and hope for tomorrow. We have a goal — to fulfill the calling of God on our lives. To reach that goal we have to remember where we find strength and hope, and where to go when we feel like we're running low.

If anyone had an overwhelming ministry call, it was Paul. After Paul's conversion on the Damascus road, the Lord spoke to Ananias about Paul's future. He said, "he is a chosen instrument of mine, to carry my name before the Gentiles and kings and the children of Israel. For I will show him how much he must suffer for the sake of my name" (Acts 9:15–16). Most of the rest of the New Testament is about how Paul fulfilled that mission. He carried Christ's name to hundreds during his life, and millions through his contributions to our Bibles. And he suffered.

> ▣ Read 2 Corinthians 11:23-28 and list some of the ways Paul said he suffered.

But still his ministry continued. He was the one who wrote, "We do not lose heart. Though our outer nature is wasting away, our inner nature is being renewed day by day" (2 Corinthians 4:16). Let's look at how Paul kept focused on his ministry and his spiritual growth.

In Philippians 3:12–14 Paul wrote, "Not that I have already obtained this or am already perfect, but I press on to make it my own, because Christ Jesus has made me his own. Brothers, I do not consider that I have made it my own. But one thing I do: forgetting what lies behind and straining forward to what lies ahead, I press on toward the goal for the prize of the upward call of God in Christ Jesus."

Paul knew he still had room to grow in spiritual maturity. He hadn't reached his goal yet. He hadn't completed his ministry.

In Romans 7:15 Paul stated, "For what I am doing, I do not understand. For what I will to do, that I do not practice; but what I hate, that I do." It is shocking Paul is saying he's not perfect, that he has a long way to go as a Christian. Think about it, this is Paul, a man who preached hundreds of sermons, started many churches, performed miracles, led many people to Jesus, and wrote two-thirds of the New Testament. We all look at Paul and think, "Wow, he's a super Christian." But Paul says, "I am not there yet, I haven't obtained the goal."

What is the goal Paul is after? Romans 7:12 tells us, "that I may lay hold of that for which Christ Jesus has laid hold of me." Paul said in Romans 8:29, "For whom He foreknew, He also predestined to be conformed to the image of His Son, that He might be the firstborn among many brethren." God saves us for the purpose of conforming us to the image of His son Jesus Christ. Being in the grip of God means you are being conformed into the likeness of Jesus Christ. The goal of Paul is to become more like Jesus, to become conformed to the image of Jesus Christ.

In Philippians 3:7, Paul said all these things he has counted loss. Paul had looked at his past successes and failures and realized those things did not define who he was. He was defined by his relationship with Jesus Christ. You are called to forget the past mistakes. Someone once said, "It is hard to move forward for Jesus if you are always looking back." Think about how ineffective you would be if you were trying to drive your car down the street, but you were looking only in your rearview mirror. Your car is going forward but you are looking at what is behind you. You are not going to get very far before you crash!

Paul said it's time for you to put the past in the past. Lee was a history major in college and taught seven years of high school history courses. He would always tell his students, "If you do not learn from your past mistakes, then you are doomed to repeat them." Learning from

your past and living in your past are two
different things.

? The special-needs journey can cause
guilt for so many of us. We wish we
would have noticed the signs sooner.
We worry we didn't try enough
therapies. We second-guess decisions
we made. Like Paul, we need to learn
from our pasts but not dwell on them.
Is there something you need to leave
in your rearview mirror today? A
burden from the past you need to stop
carrying with you?

Thinking about his past led Paul to want
to reach forward, to press on in growing in his
faith. In verse 14, Paul stated, "I press toward the
goal for the prize of the upward call of God in
Christ Jesus." The phrase "press on" means to
put forth continuous effort, to pursue the goal of

Christlikeness. This was Paul's goal — to become more and more like Jesus Christ. Where did Paul get this strength to press on? He stated in verse 14, "in Christ Jesus." Paul's strength, his power to keep going, came from his relationship with Jesus, not his own efforts. Simply put, God was giving him the power to live the Christian life.

Peter said in 2 Peter 1:2-3, "Grace and peace be multiplied to you in the knowledge of God and of Jesus our Lord, as His divine power has given to us all things that pertain to life and godliness, through the knowledge of Him who called us by glory and virtue." Peter said God has given us all the ability to live the Christian life, to do everything God has called us to do. This means in pressing on, you have the God-given power to do it!

Paul was not pressing on for himself. He wasn't pressing on for a good and comfortable life. Paul was pressing on to become more and more like Jesus Christ. When does a Christian become perfectly like Christ? When is the race over? Where is the finish line? We find in Philippians 3:20-21 that "our citizenship is in heaven, and from it we await a Savior, the Lord Jesus Christ, who will transform our lowly body to be like his glorious body, by the power that enables him even to subject all things to himself." Paul stated when you arrive in heaven you are transformed to be perfectly like Jesus Christ!

? How does knowing that your circumstances and situation are really your ministry affect your outlook? How do you find encouragement from Paul's ministry to press on in your life?

Press on, do not give up! Press on! Keep striving to be more and more like Jesus Christ everyday! And know that He will give you the strength and hope to meet each day head on.

Conclusion

We are so thankful you took this journey with us. We hope and pray you better understand the grip God has on your life. One of our favorite quotes from *The Jesus Storybook Bible* is this: God loves His children with a "Never Stopping, Never Giving Up, Unbreaking, Always and Forever Love." That's the love He has for you. That's the love He has for your child. It's because of that love we have confidence in His grip.

Like David, trust that God is always there.

Like Peter, step out in His power.

Like the bleeding woman, go to Him to meet your deepest needs.

Like the disciples, see the purpose in disabilities.

Like Christ, forgive when others hurt you.

Like Aaron and Hur, lift others up.

Like Mephibosheth, trust in God's provision for you and your future.

And like Paul, press on in the ministry God has called you to.

"Blessed is the man who remains steadfast under trial,
for when he has stood the test he will receive the crown of life,
which God has promised to those who love him."
James 1:12

About the Authors

Lee and Sandra Peoples are the parents of three boys, one with autism and one they are in the process of adopting from Ethiopia. They live in Pennsylvania, where Lee is a pastor and Sandra works as a free-lance editor and writer. They both earned Master of Divinity degrees from Southeastern Baptist Theological Seminary in 2007. Lee and Sandra view the special-needs community as their mission field and are active in their local autism support group.

You can find Sandra blogging at her personal site, sandrapeoples.com, and her editing site, NextStepEditing.com. Sandra writes for the special-needs parents' website, Not Alone (www.specialneedsparenting.net). She is also the special-needs writer for The MOB Society (www.themobsociety.com), a site for boy moms. You can find her on Twitter (@sandrapeoples), Facebook (SpeechlessbySandra), and Instagram (SandraPeoples).

Lee writes about connecting faith to everyday life on his site, leepeoples.com. He is also on Twitter (@leepeoples) and Instagram (LeePeoples).

Notes

i Greg Lucas, *Wrestling with and Angel: A Story of Love, Disability, and the Lessons of Grace* (Cruciform Press, 2010), 72.

ii Pete Wilson, *Plan B: What Do You Do When God Doesn't Show Up the Way You Thought He Would?* (Nashville: Thomas Nelson, 2009), 61.

iii Wilson, *Plan B*, 34.

iv Wilson, *Plan B*, 38.

v John Piper, "Power in Weakness" in *Be Still My Soul*, ed. Nancy Guthrie (Wheaton, IL: Crossway, 2010), 152.

vi Wilson, *Plan B*, 81.

vii Nancy Guthrie, *Hearing Jesus Speak into Your Sorrow* (Carol Stream, IL: Tyndale House, 2009), 71.

viii Amy Julia Becker, *A Good and Perfect Gift: Faith, Expectations, and a Little Girl Named Penny* (Bloomington, MN: Bethany House, 2011), 141.

ix Guthrie, *Hearing Jesus Speak into Your Sorrow*, 28.

x J. I. Packer, "Hoped-for Healing" in *Be Still My Soul*, ed. Nancy Guthrie (Wheaton, IL: Crossway, 2010), 136.

xi Guthrie, *Hearing Jesus Speak into Your Sorrow*, 32.

xii Amy Fenton Lee, *Leading A Special Needs Ministry: A Practical Guide to Including Children and Loving Families* (Orange Press, 2013), 3.

xiii Martyn Lloyd-Jones, "The Test of Crisis" in *Be Still My Soul*, ed. Nancy Guthrie (Wheaton, IL: Crossway, 2010), 92.

xiv Dustin Shramek, "Waiting for the Morning during the Long Night of Weeping" in *Suffering and the*

Sovereignty of God, eds. John Piper and Justin Taylor (Wheaton, IL: Crossway, 2006), 177.

[xv] C. S. Lewis, *The Quotable Lewis*, eds. Wayne Martindale and Jerry Root (Wheaton, IL: Tyndale House, 1989), 238.

[xvi] "New Data Shows Half of All Children with Autism Wander and Bolt from Safe Places," Autism Speaks, accessed August 30, 2013, http://www.autismspeaks.org/news/news-item/new-data-shows-half-all-children-autism-wander-and-bolt-safe-places.

[xvii] R. C. Sproul, "Senseless Tragedy?" in *Be Still My Soul,* ed. Nancy Guthrie (Wheaton, IL: Crossway, 2010), 47.

[xviii] Philip Yancey, "The Gift of Pain" in *Be Still My Soul,* ed. Nancy Guthrie (Wheaton, IL: Crossway, 2010), 29.

[xix] John Calvin "The Light of Divine Providence" in *Be Still My Soul*, ed. Nancy Guthrie (Wheaton, IL: Crossway, 2010), 52.

[xx] Corrie Ten Boom, "Just What You Need, Just in Time," in *Be Still My Soul*, ed. Nancy Guthrie (Wheaton, IL: Crossway, 2010), 122.

[xxi] Joni Earackson Tada, "Hope . . . the Best of Things," in *Suffering and the Sovereignty of God,* eds. John Piper and Justin Taylor (Wheaton, IL: Crossway, 2006), 196.

[xxii] Lucas, *Wrestling with an Angel*, 40-41

37702266R00057

Made in the USA
Columbia, SC
01 December 2018